Marriage On The Rock

Reignite the FIRE in your Relationship

Reclaim What is Rightfully Yours

J. S. PARKER

Copyright © 2016 J. S. PARKER

All rights reserved.

DEDICATION

This Book Is Dedicated To All The Men And Women Out There Who Wants Reignite the Burning Fire Back Again In Their Relationship.

CONTENTS

1. Introduction: Reignite Your Relationship — 8
2. Chapter 1: Five Keys To FIRE Up Your Relationship — 14
3. Chapter 2: Secret Key 1 – Making A Game-Time Decision — 26
4. Chapter 3: Secret Key 2 – Know & Share Your Turn-Ons — 39
5. Chapter 4: Secret Key 3 – Maintain The Mystery — 52
6. Chapter 5: Secret Key 4 – Change It Up — 65
7. Chapter 6: Secret Key 5 – Connecting On All Sexual Cylinders — 74
8. Conclusion: Congratulations! You've Reached Your Peak — 83

INTRODUCTION

REIGNITE YOUR RELATIONSHIP

Carol and Alex have been together for seven years now, and yet it feels like twenty. Their son is in kindergarten, and the baby is just at the age where she's getting into everything. Outside of his full-time job as a contractor, Alex acts as a handyman on the side in hopes of saving the down payment for a new home. Carol telecommutes from home so she can be there for the kids and avoid the high cost of daycare. Although Carol and Alex are emotionally bonded, their sex life leaves much to be desired—

literally. What started out as "hot and heavy," is now a weekend quickie between HBO and streaming Facebook.

Even though Alex and Carol agree their sexual relationship needs a reboot, they have no idea how to recapture their initial fire. They have managed to have sex a few times a month, but more times than not, it's more duty than dazzling. At first, they tried to reassure one another by promising sex tomorrow, when they'd had more sleep or when the kids went to grandmas. The problem was, tomorrow never came.

What Carol and Alex need are some help building a fire beneath their waning sexual relationship. At this point, it's going to take more than a match stroke over kindling to reeve up their sexual appetites. This one's going to need a "five-star" fire up—or should I say a "Five Key" fire up? Can you relate? Before you've finished reading about the "Five Keys," you and your partner will be sitting down this book and giving each one of them a try.

Between these pages, we will present proven strategies and practices designed to get you back on track to an incredible sexual relationship. After reading this book, you'll be wanting more—sex, that is. These Five Keys will give you so much fire in your sex life that you'll soon burn through all those bad habits you've created and release your inner sexual beast.

Oh, that got your attention, didn't it? If you found yourself shaking your head in agreement when hearing of the decrease in sexual appetite between Carol and Alex, you'll be encouraged to know that most all decreases or dysfunctions are fixable. Your sexual issues might be caused by completely different things, but the pain and hurt suffered from the lack of good sex are the same. These "Five Keys" will not only examine what could be causing your problems but will also give you practical "how to" steps to take you and your partner to a whole new sexual high. By believing in and embracing the Five Keys to light up your sexual experiences, you can expect...

- More intimacy in your relationship

- Better communication of your needs and wants

- Greater physical prowess

- Closer emotional connection

- More confidence and self-esteem

- Fewer suspicions and doubts regarding your partner

- More energy and sexual desire

- Better overall health and well-being

- Flat out—more hot sex

These five powerful Keys to reigniting your sexual fires will teach you how to reset your sexual expectations. You'll begin to see yourself as a dynamic lover and nurturing partner. As we break down each Key element to reigniting your sexual fires, you'll discover more creative and mysterious ways to please your partner and yourself. They'll teach you how to build anticipation for your next sexual encounter. Who knows, you and your lover will probably adopt this as your next "in bed" read.

Communication is everything, including how you speak with your body as well as your words. Powerful physical messages can be sent without ever saying a word. Like a moth to a flame, your partner will soon want to see what this new you is all about. As you learn more about yourself, you'll be able to more effectively communicate to your partner what to do to make you tremble with anticipation.

Notice, so far, we've talked about "building" the fire. Like every fire, it begins with a spark of promise, interest, and curiosity. To build a true fire, that spark must be tended to, fanned, and heaped with materials to create a rising flame. If you fail to tend to the fire constantly, it goes out. If you cover the fire with the sands of judgment, stress, doubt, and fear, your fire will be distinguished before it's had a chance to heat up your sex life.

Before you know it, instead of giving a stranger that sexually charged look or experience that fiery glow from an eye-to-eye light from a passer-by, you'll be eagerly waiting in the bedroom for your lover to come to bed—if you make it to the bedroom. The

Keys will provide playful and exciting ways to motivate yourself and your partner to engage in more creative sex. I'm not talking about the legs-over-your-head kind of sex unless of course, that's your turn-on. I'm talking about ways that engage your mind as well as your body. The Keys show you how to be fully committed—how to give sex the full-Monty treatment.

From learning to please yourself to giving the "let's have hot sex" signal to your partner, discovering the importance of timing and mounting anticipation is crucial. There are perfect times to have sex, and then there are perfect times to have naughty sex. There are proper places to have sex, and then there are under-the-table places to share hidden sexual activities. Having fun and being creative is not an option; it's a necessity.

So, are you "up" for this? You will be, especially when you learn these Five Keys and apply them to your sex life.

CHAPTER 1

FIVE KEYS TO FIRE UP

Before presenting the Five Keys to reignite the fire in your relationship, we wanted you to know that you are not the only one, or only couple, to have issues when it comes to losing your initial passion. Recent studies tell the real story: More than 1/3 of women between the ages of 18 to 59 years old suffer from a lack of desire for sex (1). Women are not the only ones experiencing problems in their sex lives. Sixty-two percent of men today say no to sex more frequently than women (2). We've lost our drive! It's not that most of can't enjoy sex or can't perform, it's that most of us just don't want to have sex.

Perhaps the sex we've been having hasn't left us wanting more of the same.

Of course, a decrease in your sex drive can be caused by a number of medical reasons, such as depression, high blood pressure, medications, increased stress hormones, and low testosterone levels, among other things. Or, decreased sex drives can be correlated to low energy levels, over-crowded schedules, family distractions, abusive backgrounds, or poor past experiences with sex. Some with medical issues or deep emotional scars may need to consult with a professional sex therapist or physician to regain healthy functioning.

The first thing you need to do is admit you have a sexual problem. No, you don't have to go to a meeting, introduce yourself to the group, and tell them all about your sexual dysfunction. Although I'm sure there's an encounter group for that, as well. It might be less stressful and more enlightening to examine some of the things that could be causing your low libido. Keep in mind, the reasons for a decreased sex drive can be much different between men and women.

Why Is There No Fire in Your Relationship?

To many women, sex seems somewhat unimportant; you might say it's low on their "to-do" list. Women who display these rather lackluster emotions toward sex certainly don't flip the fire switch for their partners. Emotional detachment to sex sucks all the energy out of the act. Many men who lack desire for sex can usually link their doused fire to job-related stress, money worries, and repeated rejection. Having sex then becomes robotic and routine; there just isn't enough return on the emotional or physical investment.

Here are some of the most common reasons both men and women have given for decreases in their sexual desires.

- Fear of being judged or criticized
- No more emotional connection
- Just another chore
- Too many interruptions
- Too much on their mind

- Don't have the energy
- Resentment from sex being used as a commodity
- Not enough tenderness or intimacy
- Boring—they've done it all
- He/she takes me for granted
- No fun
- Feelings of unattractiveness
- They'd rather relax in front of the television
- Unsatisfied with physical appearance
- Painful
- Sex is perceived as wrong or sinful
- Previously abusive relationship
- No foreplay—just hop on, hop off, roll over

- Been too long and now they feel awkward

- Partner never initiates sex (3)

The list of reasons for a decreased sex drive is infinite. Then there's the question of boring sex; you're having sex frequently, but it's not that hot, passionate sex that used to make you want to climb out of your skin. To some degree, that's to be expected. It's not that familiarity breeds contempt—it's more like regular sex with the same person can cause complacency. It's a proven fact that people have an instinctive need for newness. We prefer new cars to ones that have given us great service. We want new clothes over those that are more comfortable. Deep within us, we fantasize about the excitement of new partners. Unfortunately, when a new partner is found, it isn't long before that same old bedfellow "boredom" comes to call.

Some men and women are far too patient, putting up with little to no sex for years. What if it's too late to start a fire in your relationship? Put your mind to rest. It's never too late to become a more excitingly sexual person. Even if you cannot reignite the fire in this relationship, learning these Five Keys can help you to build within yourself, and that will certainly get your partner's attention. There is no list of signs that will tell you when your sex drive is waning—you are already experiencing the one most glaring sign—no sex.

So, what are the Five Keys to reignite the fire in your relationship? We thought you'd never ask!

The Five Keys to Reignite the Fire in Your Relationship

We'll go into greater detail later, but for right now I'll introduce the keys and briefly describe their meaning.

Key #1: Making a Game-Time Decision

If you have known for a long time that your relationship was blowing a bit cold, you have a decision to make. Putting the fire back into a relationship doesn't just happen by accident. To create a fire from embers takes a conscious decision and firm resolve to make it happen.

Key #2: Know & Share Your Turn-ons

Many people don't know what really turns them on because they've never exposed themselves. Not that kind of expose! They've never explored their own bodies to understand what turns them on. Being familiar with your "boiling" points is important to know, and to share with your partner. It's especially important if your turn-ons are a bit out of the norm. We'll examine some of those in a later chapter.

Key #3: Maintain the Mystery

Part of that newness we spoke of earlier comes from the fact that a new partner holds mysteries that have yet to be unfolded. We haven't been privy to their private habits that can be a buzz kill to sexual desire. We don't know their secrets, but we look forward to uncovering each tantalizing detail. For this reason, you need to reserve some things for your mystery treasures—to be unburied by your partner.

Key #4: Change It Up

When considering change, it's necessary to broaden your experiences. About all the sexual changes some people experience is the "I'll be on top this time" sort. This key will show you how to create such change that your partner will be anticipating what's to come every time you plan (and planning is an essential element) to have sex.

Key #5: Connecting On All Sexual Cylinders

This Key teaches you how to be all-in. You'll discover the incredible heat from a fire that's been fueled by employing all the Keys. Once you have a menu of choices and throw in the emotions felt from a bonded partner, you'll feel explosively energetic releases.

We've made some pretty ambitious promises, but let me share with you the reasoning behind this knowledge. There are some biological reasons why these Keys build more passionate lovemaking. No matter what your issues are, learning and practicing these Keys will give you much hotter sexual experiences. However, before you try all these things, you need to rule out a medical condition that could be an underlying, or even primary, issue.

Medical Reasons for a Decrease in Sexual Desire

You would think we'd be over the shame and stigma attached to a decline in sexual drives or having issues with sexual dysfunction. Unfortunately, this is not the case, especially for men. Men identify with their ability to perform, considering themselves to be less of a man if they aren't able to maintain an erection, or if they have little desire for sex. Although the feelings are different for women, they are no less damaging to their chances of having hot sex. Many women freely talk to other women about feeling sexually obligated or about giving their partner's sex to get something they want in exchange. It becomes a standing joke in female circles that so-and-so must be great in bed to have earned that new car or exciting trip. Exchanging sex for treats reduces passionate sex to how you would reward a dog for being obedient.

Before we begin discussing the medical and psychological issues that can put out the flame, let's agree to remove the shame or stigma from any problem you might be having. After all, if you had diabetes or high blood pressure, you wouldn't be ashamed, would you? Once the inferior feelings are forgotten, you can get started on overcoming any medical issues that could be the root cause of your inability to have or enjoy great sex.

Two of the most common medical problems that negatively affect your sex life are diabetes and high blood pressure. Females also have a whole other set of issues with the onset of menopause when their hormones tank and the walls of their vagina become thinner and more easily irritated. Younger women can also have hormonal issues when they are breastfeeding. This, however, is not a complicated fix. Most of the time, with a slight change in hormones, they are back to hot sex.

People who have thyroid problems or issues with chronic depression are also susceptible to lower sex drives. If you have nerve damage brought on by Parkinson's, multiple sclerosis, or have had pelvic surgery, these things can impact your ability to enjoy or want sex (4).

All these issues can be improved or eliminated by consulting with and following the advice of a professional. Let's examine some things you can do to improve your sex drive.

Things You Can Do to Improve Your Sex Drive

1. Get plenty of sleep.

A study done by the University of Chicago revealed that people who sleep less than five hours a night for an extended period will experience the testosterone levels of someone 15 years older (2).

2. Reduce stress.

Stress hormones like cortisol and adrenalin cause resistance to testosterone. Dr. Malcolm Carruthers, founder of the Centre for Men's Health, says: *"I do believe testosterone deficiency is becoming more common and happening younger. It used to affect mostly men in their 50s, but it's now men in their 40s and even their 30s (2)."*

3. Reduce or eliminate the use of alcohol and drugs.

It also helps to lay off the cigarettes.

4. Eat well and maintain a healthy weight.

    Carrying additional belly fat can block testosterone.

5. If sex is painful for you, don't always make it about intercourse. Spend more time enjoying the foreplay. Also, try different positions. You may find some more comfortable and less painful than others. It's always a good idea to empty your bladder before sex as well (5).

It's easy to know when to contact a professional. The answer is—right away. Don't wait for years to pass without enjoying great sex. Avoid letting physical issues create emotional stress on you and your partner.

When you've cleared up any medical reasons that may be prohibiting your ability to reignite the fire in your relationship, then it's time to move on to the five most important Keys that can help you put the heat back into your sex life.

CHAPTER 2

SECRET KEY #1

MAKING A GAME-TIME DECISION

Obviously, you have a decision to make. This Key can be the most difficult one used to unlock the secrets to lighting that fire in your relationship. The longer you have let your sex life cool, the more difficult it will be to heat things up. Although the decision will be yours to make, you will need open communications and full cooperation with your partner as well. It's a two-fold issue: (1) making the decision; and (2) getting your partner on board with your plan.

You'll notice I have referred to this process as a "game-time" decision. Let me explain what I mean by that term. A game-time decision is usually one made just at the time of play—at the exact time things need to happen. All the preparation has gone into making the decision, and then it is time to jump in and start the game. That's what it's going to be like to begin using the Keys for improving your sex life. All the preparation in the world isn't going to make that moment you decide to jump in any less awkward or stressful. What it will do is give you the courage and confidence that you are doing the right thing.

So, let's examine all the elements of preparation that will lead up to your game-time decision. You'll need to take into consideration the following points before communicating your plan to your partner.

Prepare for that Game-time Move

Deciding to embrace the Keys to hot sex is no easy endeavor. It's important to consider the elements that make up good decision-making strategies. The success of this plan could mean a rescued relationship. Don't be fooled into believing that hot sex is always spontaneous. That's the Hollywood version, where people are ripping their clothes off as they come through the door. Not that you won't want to try that strategy later on, but let's get you through the awkwardness first. That way you'll be ready to step up your game as you have some success under your belt—literally.

Taking the time to plan your decision to have great sex with your partner won't take the fun out of it, it will turn up the heat. When you've both planned to make your sex exciting, your anticipation will be a huge payoff. So, these are the elements to consider before making your game-time decision.

Uncertainty

Expect, at first, to feel hesitant and uncertain, insecure and uncomfortable. That's what this is all about, to get you out of your comfort zone. If you don't feel these emotions, you haven't created enough change to bring on the heat, to build the fire. Every time couples try new things, every time you get closer to the fire, there's a chance you'll get burned. That's part of the excitement—taking that chance. So, welcome the insecurity and discomfort; it means you are well on your way to having better sex than you've ever experienced.

Complexity

Many factors will come into play during your decision to reignite the fire in your relationship. Often, the factors that you have to consider will play against one another. For example, you will need to set aside time to build the fire. To do that, it may mean a significant change in your personal schedule, or time taken from other activities to devote to sex. Make your decisions with a clear understanding of how one issue will affect others, then prioritize. What is most important? What will have the greatest impact on your relationship? Somedays hot sex is going to take priority. Somedays, maybe not. However, if sex never comes first, if you consider sex as something to do to appease your partner when there's nothing better going on, it will eventually make you not want to play.

Consequences

There are going to be consequences to the decisions you make; every decision has its consequences—some good, some bad. What you need to do is be prepared for those consequences. For example, if you decide to role-play, or incorporate adult toys into your new sexual explorations, your partner may not agree or understand your need. Just beginning to have more sex may be a bit of a shock. So, understand that with each decision to step up your game, there will be some consequences. If you decide to build some fear of discovery into your sex life, the consequence might be that you could get caught. If that consequence isn't real, the fear won't be there.

The more creative you become when you use these Keys, the greater your results will be as well. Your response to these consequences will depend on your perception. How do you view the word consequence? A consequence is not good or bad in itself. It's simply what happens as a result of the decisions you make. All you want to do is be able to reasonably predict the consequences of your decisions. This ability to predict leads us to the next element of decision-making.

Reasonably Predict the Outcome

If you have properly considered all your options and consequences, you should have a reasonable idea of the results of your decision. When it comes time to jump in—to make that game-time decision, you'll be prepared for what could happen. Not to say the unexpected doesn't sometimes throw you a curve ball, but being able to reasonably predict the outcome of your decision will give you the confidence to handle the unexpected.

Being on your game means that you will, at times, have to make more game-time decisions. That's okay, this very first decision to jump in will prepare you for other decisions to come.

Plan Your Approach

Postponing your decision to just "do it" until the perfect time, is the coward's way out, and it's no way to reignite the heat. There is no perfect time. It's a game-time decision; the time is right now. However, how you plan to approach your partner needs some preparation. The reason you need a strategy is that all these things will come into play when communicating your needs with your partner and getting him or her to become a player as well. Building a fiery relationship is a dual effort. You cannot create the heat all by yourself. So, let's discuss how you will approach your partner.

Set the Scene

Discussing your sexual desires with your partner can be quite intimidating, so set the scene. Timing is everything. Don't wait until you're in a heated argument about your partner's inattentiveness or time spent with other people or things to bring up needing to build more fire in your relationship. Doing this will start the process off with a raging, out-of-control fire, and not usually one that lends itself to having great sex. Anger and resentment often act as fire extinguishers. Since you are the one taking the initiative to build this fire, you need to make sure the winds of discontent aren't blowing so hard that it threatens to either put your fire out or level the city. Setting the scene puts you in control.

When you're setting the stage to discuss your sexual needs, create a time and place where your voice will be heard. Make it a time when you have can freely talk about what you want to do for your partner, explaining in sexy detail how you plan to make your partner feel. Remind your lover how things used to be, how hot your sex was when you first met. In fact, bringing up a particularly exciting sexual exchange is an excellent way to get your partner's attention. See what I mean? If properly planned, the conversation alone can be a turn on.

Explore Together

Once you have made yourself vulnerable by sharing what it is you want, get your partner to join in the game. Ask them about their wants and needs. Exploration means sharing the fantasies as well as the practical ideas. During this time of exploration, make it a "no-holds-barred" kind of thing. Anything goes! Keep in mind, you've been planning this for a while, but your partner hasn't. He or she may also be struggling with insecure, uncertain feelings that might surface during your exploration of the possibilities of bringing back the fire. Again, use all your emotions to stimulate and excite one another.

It's strange how our minds and bodies react to the unknown. Most of us fear the unknown. Let me share something with you about fear. The physiological feelings one experiences with fear are the same as one experiences when you exchange a spark of interest with a stranger. When your central nervous system has been awakened, your sexual arousal will follow suit (6). The feelings of fear and arousal within your body are the same. The body doesn't know the difference; so, creating a bit of fear can be used to stimulate you and your partner's physical responses during the conversation you are having.

Now add touch to the equation, and what you have is the beginnings of a fire, my friend. As you are having this conversation, make sure you are sitting close, touching your partner. At first, the touch can be reassuring, and then see where things go from there.

Create A Vision

Decide ahead of time what you want to happen after having this conversation. If you want it to lead to hot sex, make it happen. Jump in! It could be a game-time decision that will depend on all the factors and options you have already considered. The beauty of being a visionary is that having that picture and being able to predict the outcome.

I'm sure you've heard of athletes who imagine their successful throw of a football or see themselves making a perfect trajectory of the basketball to the hoop. That's what I'm talking about. Create a picture in your mind where you want this conversation to go, and then do what it takes to turn that picture into reality. If you want it to lead to hot sex, create the possibility. If you've communicated the fact that you want to use some sex toys or that you would welcome incorporating some hot videos into your sexual activities, then have those things ready and available.

As you are having the conversation with your partner, explaining some of the things you'd like to do, let them know you have those things ready. Perhaps you could even show them what you have in mind as you're talking. All the while you are having this conversation, keep touching and talking. It's like an adult show and tell, don't you think? It won't be a secret to how your partner is responding to your conversation. You'll hear and see the fire grow until the conversation leads to the act.

Be open to where the conversation takes you. If you have set the scene for building a great fire, explored your options with your partner, and helped them to feel the heat by creating a vision through the senses, then enjoy the sex. The worst thing to do is cry or become angry if your partner doesn't respond the way you thought her or she would. Have a screaming match and storming out will make it that much harder to achieve your goal of reigniting the fire in your relationship. You've set yourself up for failure if you sit in your usual TV spots during a football game, agree to turn the sound down but leave the picture on, and clinically talk about your lackluster sex. It's almost a sure thing that after that kind of conversation, you'll have nothing to look forward to but the outcome of the game. If this is how you set the scene, then you've just tried to build your fire in the middle of a torrential downpour. It ain't gonna happen!

Some people decide to use the vision approach first. They set the scene and plan on further exploration by creating an atmosphere of surprise. The story of Tasha and Derrick will illustrate what I mean.

Tasha and Derrick had been dating for five years, and they had both slipped into the comfort and ease of Saturday "honey dos" and Sunday afternoon sports. Their routine was comfortable and pleasant, but they lacked heat in the romantic department. It's not that they didn't have sex, but it always seemed to follow that same easy, comfortable path as the rest of the time they spent together.

Sometimes Derrick and Tasha would decide to watch the football game at the neighbors. If it was a late game, Tasha would sneak out a little early, light up the grill, and have a few burgers or hot dogs ready for dinner when Derrick returned home. This Sunday she decided things were going to be a bit different. Tasha was going to light a fire, but it wasn't going to be for hamburgers. Tasha had made a decision to create some heat in her and Derrick's relationship, and she had planned well ahead of time.

Instead of hamburgers and hotdogs, Derrick came home to a darkened room with burning candles, some large, vibrating toys and an erotic video laying on the coffee table. Next, he saw Tasha standing before him dressed in hot pink lingerie. The communications were clear; there was no need for conversation. Not only had Tasha planned and set the scene, but she already had a good idea of how her partner would react.

The evening was a great success, and it led to some intimate conversation afterward. Sometimes the sex comes before the talk. It all depends on your plan. The Key is to make the decision to create the heat, and then make a plan that serves that purpose. If the unexpected happens, don't let that stop you from dropping back and huddling together to decide where to go from there. A different outcome than you planned doesn't have to be a game-stopper. Try a different approach; that's all.

CHAPTER 3

SECRET KEY #2

KNOW AND SHARE YOUR TURN-ONS

You can't share what you don't know. Before you can clearly communicate what makes you hot, you have to take a little self-inventory of your turn-ons. To give you some direction during your discovery process, we have listed some of the most common things that men and women say turns them on. Let's begin with ten things most men say are their hot buttons:

Ten Things Women Do That Make Men Hot

1. Men found it sexy when women take the initiative. If you're always the one to want sex, it can make you feel needy and undesirable. Knowing that your lady is looking at you with lust in her eyes is quite erotic. Everybody likes to feel wanted, and nothing sends that message better than a, well let's just put it bluntly, horny woman. If the decision to have sex is always initiated and led by the man, it's often difficult for the male to know if it is something his partner wanted to do

or if she's just complying to get it over with so she can watch her favorite television program.

The one who initiates sex also has a greater responsibility to make sure it's good. After all, you say to yourself; my partner is the one who wanted to do this—now, it's up to them to make me feel good. Having your partner hot for you takes the weight off your shoulders and lets you sit back and forget about all your cares and responsibilities. It sets your mind free and allows you to focus on all the pleasure your partner is giving you. Not that it is like this all the time, and that's the beauty. But, wow! Who wouldn't like to have those roles changed every once in a while?

2. Men loved their women to wear sexy lingerie or dress the part of the seductress. One gentleman said his partner would do her housework around him in nothing but a thong and stilettos. When I asked him if she ever got tired of walking around the house cleaning in high heels, he laughed. He eventually hired a housekeeper because her cleaning efforts never got any further than a few pushes with the vacuum and a deep bend in front of him with a dust cloth.

Sexy lingerie or skimpy underwear is nothing new as a turn on for men. Some like lingerie so see-through that it's only a hint of covering over the most important parts. Some men like for their partners to leave a little more to the imagination. Or, they like a tightly laced corset with thigh-high nylons. To make it a sure thing, you may want to look through some lingerie photos online or in a magazine together to see what fuels the fire.

3. Foreplay is just plain fun. Women are not alone in their love to practice tantalizing foreplay.

When someone else controls the foreplay, the heat can build to such a crescendo that it threatens your ability to hang on and wait for your partner to reach your ready level. Foreplay can be a number of things, and it doesn't always have to end in intercourse. Some men find it blissfully torturous to have a woman that is proficient in blue-balling. The rise and fall of arousal can build the heat to such intensity that intercourse is almost anticlimactic.

4. Then there are the rather adventurous men who said they loved to watch their woman masturbate and climax as they were instructed on what to do to themselves. They liked seeing the confidence of a woman who wasn't afraid of her sexuality and who didn't act ashamed of her body. Many men also enjoyed the power they have over their partner when they bring her to orgasm.

5. Some men liked to hear the sound of excitement from their partners. They got turned on as their partner's breathing became labored, and then

when moans escaped, their need heated up several degrees. Some liked to hear their names spoken or called out. Some wanted it loud and demanding. Others enjoyed just a hint of heat; a soft, horse released breath did the trick. Talking dirty is also an option, but for some partners that can be a definite turn-off. Make sure you define your turn-ons before putting them into play.

6. Some men enjoyed it when their partners squeezed their buttocks or their biceps in the heat of the moment, lifting themselves to the

motion of their bodies. Without exception, men said they liked their partners to actively participate, to do a little grind during the foreplay. Some even wanted their partners to guide their hands to their "hot" spots.

7. Some got turned on by a woman's sense of humor, feeling secure in the knowledge that if he made a mistake, it wasn't going to be earth shattering. It was a turn-on to know that he could let go of the stress and worry to focus on

the fun. Isn't that what sex should be—playful and fun?

8. Many men liked their partners to be creative, unafraid to have fantasy sex, willing to have sex on the beach or in their friend's home as they visited for dinner. Anything that added that extra little bit of danger and excitement was enough to turn those embers into a fire.

9. Hands down, every man loves head. There is something empowering to men to see their partner go down on them and take their manhood in their mouth. One thing to agree upon before giving head is what you want to have happen at the point of climax. That way your man won't be distracted by wondering if he should pull out or not. Giving head is an excellent way to bring your partner to peak level, and then making them wait a bit and settling down until you build the next wave of pleasure. Get up for a minute, walk around nude, stand in front of the bed and let them see your body's responses to his excitement. Then, start all over again. I'm getting hot just talking about it.

10. Most men wanted their partners to be up for anything, open to trying different ways to create hot sex. They wanted their partners to trust them enough to consider extreme fantasies and creative ways to light them up (7).

Okay, now that you know some of the things that men said turned them on, let's discuss what turns on women. Keep in mind; women are more complex creatures when it comes to their sexuality. A woman's turn-ons are often connected to emotional responses as well as their physical needs.

Ten Things Men Do That Make Women Hot

1. Women often preferred the lighter touches along their arms, down their backs, on their inner thighs, and brushed against their lips. What can be a turn-off is men who smash into their lips, open their mouths so wide they could swallow a watermelon, and cram their tongues down their throats until they are ready to choke. Even if you're having rougher sex, it never hurts to pull back and lightly appreciate her skin and lips.

2. Most women loved to have their partners run their fingers through their hair. Of course, not when she's all ready to go out, but sitting on the couch during a make-out session or foreplay, scoop her hair back and even hold it a little tighter at the nape of her neck. It's a promise of gentle yet powerful sex. Very hot, guys!

3. Not only did women love the fresh smell of their partners, but they also enjoyed the act of showering together. It can be quite hot to feel each other's slick, soapy skin. A creative

combination might be to wash your partner's hair for her while you're showering together. Now you're thinking! Spooning with your partner in the shower lets them feel the full pressure of your excitement as you run your fingers over her breasts, stomach, and down to her most private places.

4. Women found intelligence a turn-on. They liked their men to know about different things and be willing to talk about what they know. They wanted a man smart enough to challenge them

and press them to be better. The mind is probably one of the most neglected sexual parts of one's body. When your partner can capture your thoughts, you can get lost in the process.

5. Women also enjoyed being surprised. Not just presents, either, although they're certainly welcomed once in a while. Surprises come in many different packages. Sometimes a surprise could be fixing the leaking sink that you promised to do two months ago, or making arrangements to have a meal catered in one night. If you want

to make it a sexual surprise, linking it with food is always fun. The old whip-cream standby is good, then add a few strawberries and a few ice cubes from your drink, viola—you've got a hot surprise.

6. Women also loved partners who were patient with them. Don't get angry if they got home from work a little late. Avoid losing your temper with them when they take longer than you would like when it comes to putting on their makeup. Regarding foreplay, patience is a total turn-on. Wait for your partner's legs to shake and for her

begging to begin before penetration. Believe me; that will sometimes take the patience of a saint— but the heat a patient partner creates is worth the wait.

7. Seductive texting was also a turn-on for women, especially when they'd had a particularly trying day. Instead of asking them what happened, tell your partner you have a way to take her mind off her problems and you plan on showing her when she gets home. Then, make the evening be about her. Give her a massage, from her shoulders,

down her back, around to her inner thigh, and to her feet. Use a lubricant, and warm it up to warm her up.

8. Understanding a woman's personal needs will let her know that you know her inside and out. If she is grumpy, don't always think it's something you did, just give her some space. Don't worry the situation or take the blame for something with which you are probably not involved. Don't get pouty and quiet; your partner deserves the chance to express her feelings even if she's

grumpy or in a mood. Let her have those feelings, and welcome her back with open arms when she's ready to confide in you. If she doesn't feel like talking, call it good, and cuddle. With her distractions, this may not be a very good time for hot sex, but soft touches and cuddling can let her know you're sensitive to her needs.

9. Women like a well-dressed, freshly scented partner. Be careful about using cologne that's too heavy; you don't want to cover up the delicious smell of hot sex. Have you ever noticed

that? Sex has such a warm glowing fragrance to it; you may just want to use soap as a scent and then let your manliness come through. Whenever you go out, your partner is wearing you like a designer accessory. So, make her proud!

10. Most women wanted to hear about their partner's feelings and beliefs. They wanted to know they were special enough for their man to share with them their deepest thoughts and secrets. Talking in bed after sex is an excellent

time to do this. It increases the intimacy. Who knows, you could be headed for another fire (8).

You may not know yourself well enough or have enough confidence to voice your turn-ons to your partner. That's cool! The process of discovery will be eye-opening. You'll discover, and it will become quite obvious to your partner, the things that send you to the moon and back. If you can't tell your partner with words what you want, show him or her with sexy sounds and let your body speak for you at first. When you see how the Keys turn on the heat, you'll soon find the words to share with your partner all the things you want to have done to you and what you plan to do in return.

Try some of these Key things on yourself and with your partner to kick up the heat. Anticipate the amazing sex you'll have together, and share your imaginations and fantasies with your partner. Tell him or her what you plan on doing, and as you're exchanging likes and dislikes, a little bit of showing will go a long way to fan the sexual flames. All I've got to say is—enjoy the fire!

CHAPTER 4

SECRET KEY #3

MAINTAIN THE MYSTERY

Insert chapter five text here. Insert chapter five text here. Insert chapter Practicing this Key can be challenging, so let me explain what I mean by maintaining the mystery in your relationship. Can you remember how you felt about your partner when you began your relationship? You were both eager to learn about one another. It seemed like you just couldn't get enough. You weren't just hungry for their body, but you wanted to have it all—to consume and fold them into you until you knew one another's thoughts before they were spoken words.

Wanting to know everything about your partner isn't really what you desired, though. What most people seek is the "want." You want to still "want" to know more about your partner. Does that make sense? When you quit wanting more, you quit altogether. It's the desire that drives the relationship—that creates the intimacy that reignites the fire of your relationship.

Mysterious doesn't mean manipulative. Don't play games to purposefully make your partner doubt your relationship or your devotion. That's unfair and cruel, and it will end up backfiring on you in the long run. Being a bit mysterious just means holding back a little for later, saving part of yourself so that your partner enjoys the discovery process. When he or she asks you something, instead of answering, let them know that you'll tell them later. Or, talk to them about how to find the answer to that one for themselves.

Be genuine and honest with your partner when you are creating or maintaining the mystery in your relationship. Those of you who have been in a relationship for a long time are probably thinking—it's a bit late for this Key, right? Wrong! For you, instead of holding information back and being mysterious, you have to create new mystic—but how? That's Key #3.

Give Cause to Question

When I say cause to question, I don't mean for you to give your partner cause to question your devotion or loyalty. Give him or her cause to wonder what you have up your sleeve—what is coming next. Be unpredictable. Do the unexpected. Keep your partner guessing, and make it fun and playful. For example, Clair curled up with a good book one cold winter evening. The fire was going, but there was a chill in the air, so she had her flannels on and a cozy cover-up as she laid beside her sweetie on the sofa. You wouldn't exactly call her pajamas sexy, but what she did with them started to light Patrick up.

She pulled the covers up to right below her neck as she read her book. At first, Patrick didn't look to see what she was reading. In fact, he paid little attention to Clair at all. He was busy streaming Facebook and checking his emails. So, she laid her book, print down, on the table so Patrick could see that it was an erotic book. Still acting like nothing was up as she adjusted the covers; then she picked the book back up and continued to read. Only, now that he saw the cover of the book, she had captured his interest. Next, Clair pulled off the bottoms to her pajamas and began playing beneath the covers, while still holding the book. The action beneath the blanket started getting more heated, and Patrick wanted in on the action. It was a fun evening, and it wasn't long before neither Clair nor Patrick needed the covers or the fire; they were making a fire together that made the one in the fireplace unnecessary. Clair never turned a page of that book, and Patrick never noticed because he was busy under the covers with Clair.

The reason I share this story with you is that Clair did the unpredictable, and it ended in great sex. She didn't sit down to have a big talk with Patrick; she just started building the fire all by herself and Patrick joined in. What she did was peak Patrick's curiosity, and then teased him into being attentive.

There was no nagging or anger, just playful fun. Not only did Clair capture Patrick's attention, but because she has continued now and then to do the unpredictable, Patrick looks forward to what's coming next—besides him.

Another element of Clair's sofa surprise is that she kept herself hidden. What is hidden is often more enticing than what is offered in plain sight. If someone walks along a nude beach sporting a skimpy bathing suit while all the other beach people are stark naked, who do you thing gets the most attention? You guessed it, the one that left a little to the imagination.

Don't Always Be Readily Available

It may sound like you're game-playing, and perhaps in a way you are. However, it's a healthy game designed to keep the fire burning in your relationship. What I mean by not always being readily available is this. Don't wait by the phone, picking it up on the first ring, out of breath as if you ran to answer. Don't ask when your partner is going to call, just expect that he or she will. If they tell you they'll give you a call, let them know that you have plans and may not be home so they can leave a message and you'll call them back later. Now you've got them wondering where you are going, who you'll be with, and when you'll call them back. You've created some mystery.

Being needy with your partner is like pouring water on the fire. Rarely do others enjoy having to reassure someone all the time by reporting their whereabouts. Don't become an extension of your partner—get a life! Be active with friends of your own. Avoid making your partner responsible for planning your daily activities. In fact, he or she doesn't need to be included in everything you do.

Don't Talk Too Much

No matter if your relationship is new or you have years of familiarity with one another, avoid talking non-stop about every little insignificant detail of your day. Don't write on your Facebook about everything you did during the day. Although it's great to share things with your lover, does your partner need to know you just picked up a Starbuck's latte? Sometimes, it's fun to send a text to say—*"Guess where I am?"* Then don't respond when he or she returns the text. As predicted, as soon as your partner gets home, he or she will probably be asking about that text.

People who talk too much about themselves can completely shut down their partners with the same old boring chit-chat. Learn to be an attentive listener. Get your mind out of yourself and into your partner. When you talk, share things that matter to your partner—perhaps something new you discovered about his or her favorite activity, sport, or hobby. Let them know you are thinking of them.

Some Things Are Better Left to the Imagination

This is especially true if you've been together for quite some time and the fire in your relationship is only showing a few flumes of smoke—if that. What I mean by this is, when you're doing private things, to keep them private. For example, when you use the potty, shut the door. When you are coloring your hair, do it at a time when your partner is out with friends. When the "boys" are itchy, avoid spreading your legs open on the couch in front of the game and giving yourself a three-minute scratch down. Believe me, when I tell you, this is far from a fire builder. Some things are better done in private.

Most bathroom grooming should be done alone unless of course, you're using the shower as an enticement. Make the bathroom a place of sexy fun, not a place where your partner is exposed to all your daily duties. If your dog leaves the bathroom when you've entered, it's a clear sign that what routinely goes on in there needs to be private. Enough said!

Challenge Your Partner

A little healthy competition can raise the heat in a relationship. Competitive activites should be something that you enjoy together. If you have a sport that both of you participate in, make it competitive. If you don't do any activities together, you've got to challenge yourself to find one. It's important that you find activities that can be enjoyed together. It gives you something to talk about and a time of fun together. It also lets you show off your prowess and strength. If the sport is swimming, that could open up a whole new set of skills.

Challenging your lover doesn't always have to be in the form of sport. You can test them in a computer game, playing cards, or even just making a bet. Who knows, the payoff can be quite rewarding for both of you.

Let Your Partner Earn Your Compliments

Avoid fishing for compliments—it's just another way you show your insecurities. Women can be particularly guilty of this. They'll ask if they look too fat in this outfit, or become offended if their partner doesn't compliment their new hairdo or designer shoes. One lady has a unique way of knowing when her rather undemonstrative partner thinks she looks extra special. He has a dead giveaway sign that he's impressed. He raises his eyebrows when he sees her. That's all—raised eyebrows?

Yep, what this woman has learned is to recognize even the smallest signal from her partner. She knows she looks good, and she's never been one to like lavish compliments. Instead, she searches her partner's face for those telltale raised brows to celebrate her exceptional appearance. What's more, she's learned to return the favor. There have been times when they are across the room at a party, and she will give him that look, raise a dainty little brow, touch her finger to her parted lips, and build a long-distance fire that they both know won't be able to be enjoyed for a few hours. The anticipation is deliciously hot.

Encourage Silent Communication

These kinds of communications are only between the two of you, creating together the mystery that nobody else can share. These types of silent communications should be little tidbits of information to which only you and your partner are privy. For instance, you may want to whisper in your lover's ear as you go into a restaurant that you feel naked without wearing panties, or ask him to see if he thinks anyone could tell that you are not wearing a bra.

One gentleman told me of a time he was at his tennis club, and he found himself being turned on by watching his lover compete in the final round. After she had won the match, he gave her their silent signal, and together they celebrated her win in the club's darkened supply room. Everyone had left, or so they hoped, and it was just them, the linens, and that lovely musky smell of hot sex. The point is, they had a shared secret, a wonderfully mysterious way to communicate their needs that left out the rest of the world.

Create the Mystery

When you have been together for quite some time, it takes a bit more work to create mystery in your relationship. You have already shared so much information and know each other so well, that you can practically finish one another's sentences. So, you may think this Key is not going to be possible for you. Not so! It may be a little more challenging for you to create opportunities to be mysterious, but that element of surprise and the knack of being unpredictable will be your ticket to success.

Speaking of tickets, one lady shared this interesting story. She felt her partner needed a little space in their relationship. So, she bought tickets for him and a buddy to go to the football game. When she gave him the tickets, she also informed him that she'd be waiting for him when he returned with another surprise. Then she said, if the lights are out when you get home, don't sit down and snack in front of the television. Come on into the bedroom. I'll be waiting there for you with your surprise.

He was so excited thinking about what she had planned that there were times he found it impossible to focus on the game. Although his buddy wanted to stop for a drink after the game, her partner politely refused. He had better things to do.

Creating and maintaining the mystery in a relationship builds excitement and anticipation of a hot encounter. It takes planning and effort, but the results are well worth it. This, in fact, is one of the Keys that can be the most fun and playful. The fire that these sexual games put into your relationship is so memorable that just reminding your partner of them at another time will tease the senses.

I challenge you to be creative with this Key and make your sex unique and individual. Create private communications and develop an intimate language that is only understood by you and your partner.

CHAPTER 5

SECRET KEY #4

CHANGE IT UP

Although we've talked a great deal about different things you can do to build the heat, keep in mind anything you repeatedly do creates a routine. Between the games, the positions, the toys, and techniques, sometimes your partner just wants comfortable, nurturing, gentle love-making for a change. All of the Keys you use are designed to please and stimulate, but changing things up lets you excite your partner and have great sex irrespective of their attitude or mood.

To know when to play and when to put playfulness aside and just focus on body worship, you have to be able to read your partner. Being attentive and sensitive to your partner's feelings and emotions are paramount to using these Keys. Your flexibility and desire to please your partner must trump your desire to please yourself. If your partner needs to be nurtured and cuddled, then that should be your focus. If your partner needs to feel empowered, then do what's necessary to fulfill that need.

We've offered you a treasure chest of golden Keys to reignite the fire in your relationship, but being willing to change and use these Keys will determine how much heat you can create. To continue to build the fire, refuse to allow yourself to do one thing most of the time. Change things up, be creative, be unpredictable, be fun and playful, be tender, be rough—but most of all be knowledgeable about all the things you can do to keep the fire burning.

The idea of changing things up is not just a clever ploy; it's a scientific fact that people need change. Studies have shown that dopamine decreases over time with the same sexual partner. Does this mean you must find another partner? Not necessarily. Let's discuss how our dopamine levels come into play when we're feeling all the pleasures of incredible sex.

I don't mean to over-simplify, but I also don't want to reduce dopamine into a scientific discussion about neurons and transmitters, either. Dopamine is commonly called the pleasure chemical. It is that magical molecule that gladly supports all our most sinful habits and cravings, as it passes along pleasure signals to reward us when we have sex or feel lustful. Increases in dopamine keep us coming back for more. Sometimes you don't even have to have sex, just be reminded of it when smelling perfume or cologne associated with an exciting sexual encounter, and your dopamine levels begin to increase (9).

Changing it up can cause the sexual excitement that stimulates an increase in dopamine levels, making it possible to have hot sex without the need to change partners every few months. The more creative and imaginative you are when it comes to changing things up, the greater your chances will be to reignite the fire in your current relationship. Emotionally bonding with another partner takes time and energy, so why not build a sensual fire with the person to whom you are already attached?

Not only can you change things up by creating mystery and employing new devices that stimulate your imagination as well as your body, but you can change where and when you have sex as well. Once you have experimented in every room in your home, take it outside. Expand your sex to include public places where the chances of you getting caught increase your excitement. Talk about sex and get your partner aroused at a time when there is no possible way to satisfy your need for hours, and then watch the fire build. Tory and Malcolm know the value of applying this Key to their sex life.

Malcolm teased Tory late one afternoon before going to their in-laws for dinner. They showered together, getting one another quite lathered up, and then Malcolm remembered something he had to do before leaving. In a rush, with many apologies, he hoped out of the shower, leaving Tory in a state of unsatisfied heat. All the way to his in-laws, Malcolm kept saying that he was sorry and promised to make it up to her later. This only served as a reminder of what she had missed.

The whole evening, Malcolm would glance at Tory, with a promise of pleasure when they got home, and all the while Tory and Malcolm's dopamine levels were skyrocketing. Every once in a while, Malcolm would slide his hand up Tory's leg beneath the table to keep her body engaged as well as her mind. Dinner ended early that evening, and they rushed back home for a desert of a different kind.

Changing it up almost always involves some additional tools of the trade, you just need to be sure you are both in agreement with whatever activities sound interesting. If you lack imagination and creativity, watch the movie *"Fifty Shades of Grey,"* and pick up some helpful information. Not that you'll want to go to that extreme, but experimenting is allowed. While you're at it, watch the movie with your partner. It will give you a chance to build and fire and discuss your sexual likes and limits.

Tools and Toys

To help you out, we have included some interesting tools and toys to enhance your sex life. The beauty of these devices is that you can shop for them discreetly online. If you have done so, you'll be quite entertained by their variety and scope. You'll find toys that vibrate, gyrate, and pulsate. You'll find devices in all colors and textures, with ones designed to fit inside, outside, and even on your fingers. For those of you who plan on water sports, you'll be happy to know that many are toys are waterproof. If your changeup includes postponing sex and building the fire, you'll find devices that can be worn in the underwear or tucked securely inside the body that can be controlled remotely. These types of toys can create a whole other kind of mystery and secret signal, right?

Sexually stimulating toys are not just to pleasure women, but many are specially designed just for men. What used to be intimidating for men is now not only acceptable but eagerly anticipated. An online survey was done in 2014 of 5,000 men. The study was conducted to discover how men felt about the use of sex toys. They found that 51 percent of men owned sex toys, 60 percent said they had used them on their partners, and it was extremely enjoyable.

Included in these toys for men are vibrating cock rings, to contain the heated variety if that peaks your interest. There are butt plugs, and sleeve or pocket vaginas that can be filled with a wide range of excitable ingredients. If anything, just shopping for the toys can be an awesome experience for you and your partner. Shop together and double your fun. It's a great way to introduce the new possibilities, to bring up the fact that you want to increase the heat in your sex life. Just tell your partner you want to do some online shopping together for some special surprises.

For you who enjoy living on the edge, there are the extreme toys. These are used in couples' bondage games which combine pleasure with a little sting.

They include floggers, blindfolds, ropes, handcuffs, and chains. These types of toys are usually for the more seasoned sexual appetites, but having a knowledge of such activities is a good thing just in case you decide to take a giant step outside your comfort zone.

It's a good thing most people are past the idea that sex toys are weird, and boy are we past it! Adult toys in North America alone is a $500,000 a year industry, worldwide it has exploded to a multi-billion-dollar business (10). The choices are endless, and they also include lubricants, which can be purchased as all natural, organic, and water soluble products. There are lubricants that provide various sensations, like tingling, warmth, and icy cool, so you can experiment and determine which ones tickle your fancy. They come in almost any flavor under the sun or have no taste at all. Some are smooth textured, and some are granulated. So many choices—so little time.

Pricing for your sex toys is about as varied as the products, beginning as low as $5 on up to $200 plus. My point is, and I hope this important Key has demonstrated that there are so many things you can incorporate into your sex life to reignite the fire in your relationship. Some techniques or toys you may not like, but you won't know how to change it up without doing some investigating. You will know your partner's likes and dislikes better if you explore your options together, and now you can do so in the privacy of your home.

CHAPTER 6

SECRET KEY #5

CONNECTING ON ALL SEXUAL CYLINDERS

Connecting with your partner on all levels takes your experience a whole level up. No-emotion sex is good, but when you connect physically and emotionally, it's unbelievable. The more you can connect with your partner, the more you'll want to.

All the games, toys, movies, lingerie, or erotica cannot give you that "as one" connection if it doesn't come with deep emotional commitment to your partner. That's what is called connecting on all sexual cylinders.

When the heat is high and so is your emotional connection, sex becomes love-making. When your fire is burning strong, and you're implementing all the Keys you've learned, your love-making can reach euphoric heights. It takes all the Keys. You have to make a conscious decision to build the heat into your relationship. Then, discover and share your turn-ons with your partner. Be unpredictable, do the unexpected to maintain some mystery in your relationship. Get creative and be willing to change it up so that the fire doesn't die. Lastly, apply all the Keys to keep the fire going, each partner eager to experience the next sexual encounter.

This is your opportunity to transform yourself into a sexual beast. At work you may be the best nurse or lawyer, but once you get home, you can change into a pornstar. Okay, it doesn't have to be that extreme, but you will discover some additional perks when you can heat up your relationship. Great sex can change other aspects of your life as well.

Hot Sex Can Change Your Professional Prowess

When you are more confident with your sexual self, it changes your level of confidence and your ability to communicate. Let's face it, the more confident you become, the more likely you are to be valued at work. When you are perceived as a valued worker, the monetary rewards soon follow. Also, your ability to communicate is greatly enhanced with a "hotter" sex life. Why? To have a great sex life, you have to be an excellent communicator—with your body language as well as your words.

Today's workers, whether white or blue collar, deal with a tremendous amount of stress. If that pressure is allowed to build, it can turn you into a discontent complainer. Your energy level goes down, and you find yourself depressed and unhealthy. Before you realize it, you're taking more sick days or personal time, and still you feel tired. Those who allow themselves to be lackluster sexual partner soon become unenthusiastic business partners.

Hot sex also makes the participants able to concentrate and focus more at work. Once you've learned the Five Keys to reigniting your relationship, you have to get creative and be determined to put them into practice. Your focus and concentrated effort brings you great rewards, and so your brain begins to conceive of other ways to focus and concentrate. It's only natural that you take these skills to the workplace.

Also, practicing the Five Keys taps into your creative side. Even those that haven't previously considered themselves to be imaginative will be much improved after implementing the Five Keys into their relationships. That same creative effort will also spread into your career efforts, giving you the willingness to try different problem-solving strategies or office management techniques. By building the fire in your relationship, you can also create greater opportunities for success in other areas of your life.

Hot Sex Makes You More Attractive

Have you ever heard people say, *"Oh, you must have got some last night?"* Even if you didn't, why would people say that? It's because most people recognize the difference in one's appearance when they have recently had hot sex. Their skin glows. They walk taller. Their smile is wider. They're more patient. They're more accepting of new ideas. It's a commonly accepted fact that people who regularly have great sex are just more fun to be around. More people are attracted to individuals who ooze sexual energy, and you can't help but do so when you're still experiencing the aftermath of an intense sexual encounter.

I've heard it said that sexier people are more active and that increased activity helps you to be less stressed and more youthful. When you are enjoying a raging fire in your relationship, you'll want to look and feel your best outside the bedroom. Your body image will improve, and you will have a little spring in your step (11).

You'll Identify with Your Newly Discovered Sexuality

Many people who have accepted a life of boring sex or no sex at all, have learned to compartmentalize their lives. They often will share with their closest confidant that their relationship is great—all but the sex, that is. What they have done is create a separate box in which to store their unsatisfactory sex. Once tucked away, it doesn't have to cause them discomfort or embarrassment anymore. These people have become masters at disassociating their sex lives from all the other elements that make them unique.

Just as those having great sex become better all-around individuals, people who suffer the pangs of separating their souls from their sex lives begin to see the negative impact that separation can cause in their lives. Our sexual prowess has a direct correlation with our self-perception and how others see us as well. Like it or not, we are often defined by our sexuality.

If you want to experience life to its fullest, you have to do it all—including sex. It isn't all about sex, but sex is an important part of all our lives. If sex is so important to our well-being, then why settle for just "so-so" sex? Why not crank up the heat, ignite the flame of desire you once had and bring sex back to life? Nobody will appreciate it more than your partner—except maybe you.

You now have a sexual toolbox, filled with all the elements of the Five Keys. If these Five Keys are to be beneficial, you have an important choice to make. Do you finish the book and do nothing, wishing off and on you had the nerve to apply the Keys to your sex life? Or, do you get started immediately on ways to build a fire in your relationship? It's imperative to know that by saying yes to change, it will require something from you. You now have a responsibility to do the work, to keep the fire burning, to increase the heat, and to share more of yourself with your partner.

All strong people have vulnerabilities; all have weaknesses that can either be hidden or used to bring about great changes in their lives. Your sexuality carries with it great power, opportunities, and incredible rewards if you say yes to putting the Five Keys to work for you and your partner. By applying these Keys, you and your partner's lives will be enriched and energized. It won't take long, either. Just a lot of practice, but who's going to complain about having more fiery sex?

It's never too late to practice the Five Keys. If you think your relationship is too cold to try, what have you got to lose? If you or your partner is about to walk anyway, you've got nothing to lose, right? If you move on to greener pastures, you can pack up your Keys and take them with you. If you have no partner to practice them with, that's okay. You can practice alone and get to know your turn-ons that much better. If you are to have a start-over, you will know better this time around.

However, if there are still some embers burning in this relationship, try rekindling them. Even if you have some other challenges, all relationships have challenges. Guess what? Many of those challenges are caused by boring sex or no sex at all. The decision you make right now can be life altering, no kidding! Don't believe me? Give it a try—see for yourself. All it takes is a decision to apply the Five Keys and bring on the heat, in this relationship or another.

Have you decided? Good! Now turn off the television, slip into something more revealing, put down this book, and let it burn, baby.

CONCLUSION

Thank you again for purchasing this book! I hope this book was able to help you to begin reigniting the FIRE in your relationship. The next step is to master the "Five Keys" and create heat and romance by rekindling the embers and building a raging fire that renews and strengthens you and your partner.

Thank You and Good Luck!

References:

1. *Why Women Lose Interest In Sex* (www.webmd.com/sex-relationships/features/loss-of-sexual-desire-in-women), Retrieved September 23, 2016.

2. Goldwin, Clair; The Daily Mail: (2013), *Why Are So Many Men Losing Their Sex Drive?* (www.dailymail.co.uk/.../why-men-losing-sex-drive-men-likely-refuse-sex...), Retrieved September 23, 2016.

3. Franklin, Kristina, Prasse, Mike & Clemons Jr., Steven (2014), *When Intimacy Breaks Down: Reasons Many Married Women Lose Interest in Sex;* Carolinas Counseling Group, (www.carolinacounseling.info/blog/2014/11/4/epivjs6hr4rlyyxuulingmw82qf021), Retrieved September 23, 2016.

4. Sloan, Louise (2008), *Medical Reasons Why Some Women Don't Enjoy Sex* (www.health.com/SexualHealth), Retrieved September 23, 2016.

5. Medical Encyclopedia: *Women and Sexual Problems* (www.medlineplus.gov/medicalencyclopedia), Retrieved September 23, 2016.

6. Nerdlove, Dr.; *5 Ways to Bring the Spark Back to Your Relationship* (www.doctornerdlove.com/Relationships), Retrieved September 22, 2016.

7. Carter, Clint (2014), *10 Things Every Man Wants In Bed* (www.womenshealthmag.com/sex-and-love/men-want-in-bed), Retrieved September 23, 2016.

8. *30 Huge Turn-ons For a Girl* (www.love.allwomenstalk.com/huge-turn-ons-for-a-girl), Retrieved September 23, 2016.

9. Brookshire, Bethany: *What Is Dopamine? Love, Lust, Sex, Addiction, Gambling, Motivation...* (www.slate.com/.../what_is_dopamine_love_lust_sex_addition_gambling_motivation), Retrieved September 25, 2016.

10. Rosen, David (2014) *Sex Toy Industry Has Quietly Turned Into Multi-Billion-Dollar Business* (www.alternet.org/.../sex-toy-industry-has-quietly-turned-multi-billion-dollar...) Retrieved September 25, 2016.

11. Matsliah, Eyal: *Can Great Sex Transform Your Life?* (www.intimatepower.com?can-great-sex-transform-your-whole-life), Retrieved September 25, 2016.

www.ingramcontent.com/pod-product-compliance
Lightning Source LLC
LaVergne TN
LVHW012025060526
838201LV00061B/4472